This is a physical copy of the in-game manual. With future updates to the game it is possible the manual will change to reflect those updates. The game will always contain the latest version of the manual.

THE BANISHED VAULT

MMCCX

Game Manual

Nic Tringali

Art by Garin

Version 1

Production Alexander Sliwinski, Farleigh Langridge
Editing Julia Brown, Mike Bithell

For AD

Table of Contents

Introduction

The Banished Vault is a strategy game of exploration and endurance. Guide your Exiles on a journey across the stars, fleeing an unknown phenomenon known as the Gloom. Explore solar systems and travel with the Vault, a vast interstellar monastery that once was only a home and now a salvation.

The stars have been inhabited for the greater part of a millennia. Through wars, plague, and expansion, the interstellar churches have endured.

For generations, the churches strengthen their control over Stasis, a hybrid matrix that sustains life for the long hibernation of interstellar travel.

They send Vaults, vast monastery-cities built for tens of thousands, to explore and colonize new worlds.

On the fringes of territorial space, a colony mission conducted by the Auriga Vault discovers a phenomenon they christen the Gloom. It summarily annihilates the settlers, leaving behind only a meager crew of Exiles.

The Exiles flee to new solar systems. Relentlessly pursued by the Gloom, they gather resources from planets to create more Stasis, before being compelled to return to hibernation.

They resolve to undertake a new task, to write a Chronicle of their journey and transmit it home.

Escaping a solar system requires careful exploration and planning. Resources quickly grow scarce, and hazards test your Exiles' faith in the face of a cruel and infinite universe.

Your goal is Stasis, a substance that keeps your Exiles alive for the hibernation between the stars. If you survive for long enough, a Chronicle is written, as a remembrance of your journey, and your Exiles' last act.

Where To Start

To learn The Banished Vault, begin with the introductory scenarios. These scenarios are enabled with the "Tutorial Scenarios" setting when starting a new journey. The instructions for them are on pages 4 through 10.

Once you have completed the scenarios, the game presents you with a full solar system. Guidelines for completing this system are on pages 13 and 14.

After this, the full game is opened to you. The Game Concepts section explains the various concepts of the game in detail. Refer to these sections as necessary to fully understand a component of the game.

The Reference section contains specific details on the many items and elements in the game such as building costs, ship values, resources, and more.

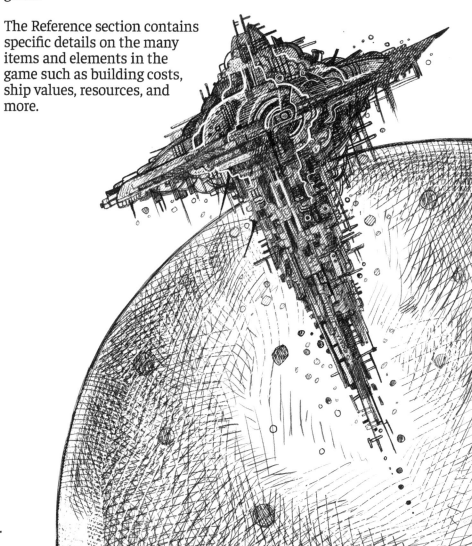

Controls

WASD	Move Camera
Left Click	Select
Right Click	Pick up 1 Cargo / Cancel
Shift + Click	Quick Swap
Mouse Wheel	Zoom
Space (hold)	End Turn
R / F1	Manual
QE	Rotate Building
Esc	Options

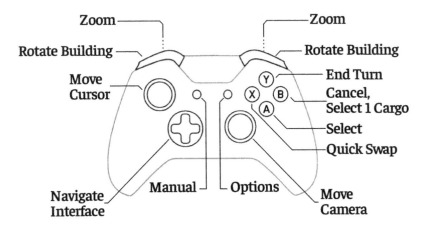

Quick Swap is a useful function to send Exiles or Cargo from ship displays to the Vault or location display, and vice versa. An Exile sent from the ship goes to an open place in the Vault or location, or swap with an Exile present. Items are sent from the storage of one space to another if there is an empty place in the destination.

Navigate Interface is a controller aid to make navigating the interface panels easier. While hovering over a button, press on the directional pad and the cursor moves to the next interface item in that direction.

Scenario 1 - Ship Maneuvers

The first scenario of the game teaches you how to move ships around a solar system and entering hibernation.

The moth fills the sky, dimming the sky to a pale fog. Days later, we notice the arc bending towards the sun.

Extract 46, dated MMCCX.14062

The first section of the scenario is to collect supplies from a stranded ship. Then, collect some Stasis already present at a planet. Finally, return your Exile and the Stasis to the Vault and begin hibernation.

View the controls for the game at any time from the pause menu.

Basic Maneuvers

To move a ship, you need to assign an Exile to be navigator, an engine, and fuel for the engine to generate Energy.

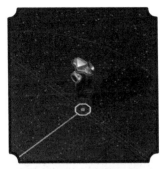

Step 1 Open Ship Display: Select the ship figurine on the map to open the display.

Step 2 Find Stranded Ship: Move the camera to locate the other ship to rendezvous with.

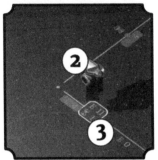

Step 3 Set Maneuver Destination: Select the map location underneath the stranded ship. This sets the destination for our maneuver, and shows the Energy needed.

Step 4 Assign Engine: On the ship display, take the engine from the cargo and place it into the Engine slot.

Step 5 Allocate Fuel: Select the right arrow button below the engine to increase the fuel used for this maneuver.

The more fuel used, the more Energy is generated by the engine. This must meet or exceed the needs for the maneuver you set.

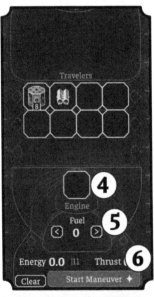

Step 6 Start Maneuver: Once you have enough fuel for the maneuver, select the Start Maneuver button.

Step 7 Turn Stop: Before the ship reaches its destination, it stops midway. These Turn Stops add time to a maneuver. The ship resumes its maneuver at the start of the next turn, so select End Turn at the top of the screen.

Continue To Landing on a Planet

Landing on a Planet

At this point in the scenario, your main ship needs more fuel and a better engine to land on the nearby planet. You'll get those items from the stranded ship.

To stand in a stellar oculus is to know the embrace of starlight.

The Eleventh Manuscript of Balthe

Step 1 View Stranded Ship: With both ships in the same location, open the ship display. You'll see an extra button representing another ship at this location. Use this button to open the stranded ship's display.

Step 2 Transfer cargo: Select the engine in the stranded ship's cargo, and then select the main ship's panel next to the display to transfer the engine. Do the same with the fuel in the stranded ship's cargo.

Step 3 Plot a Course: With the main ship, select the surface location of the planet to set a maneuver path. Note how the path between orbit and surface has a Thrust requirement.

Step 4 Assign Landing Engine: Change engines to the more powerful engine you just acquired. This engine satisfies the Thrust requirement needed to land on the planet.

Step 5 Complete Maneuver: Allocate fuel and travel to the planet's surface.

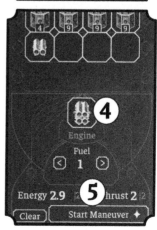

Continue to The Planet's Surface and Return

The Planet's Surface and Return

Your ship has arrived at the planet, and you are now able to view the surface. You'll retrieve the Stasis here and return to the Vault to begin hibernation.

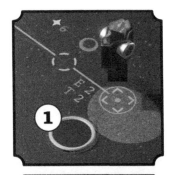

Step 1 Enter Surface View: Select the figurine on the map next to the location to enter the surface view of the planet.

Step 2 Collect Stasis: The display on the right shows the details of this location. Take the Stasis here and place it on your ship.

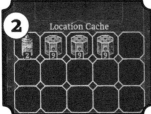

Use Quick Swap (see Controls) to quickly transfer items back to your ship.

Step 3 Return to the Map: Select the Return to Map button at the top of the display to exit the location.

Note the Vault has now appeared on the location you started the scenario.

Step 4 End Turn: Your Exile has run out of actions for this turn. Before you return to the Vault, end the turn to restore their actions.

Step 5 Return to the Vault: Plot a maneuver with your ship and return with your Exile and all resources to the Vault.

Step 6 Transfer Cargo: Select the Vault figurine to open the Vault Display. Transfer all your cargo to the Vault, and place the Exile in the Vault's crew area.

Step 7 Begin Hibernation: Select the Begin Hibernation button on the Vault to proceed to the next solar system.

End Scenario.

Scenario 2 - Construction

This second scenario teaches the basics of constructing buildings on a planet, and using them to create Stasis.

The traditional spire on the horizon of a planet has not been seen for centuries. Outposts are no longer aligned to the coordinator, and are simply pragmatically situated on a surface as necessary.

The Ritual of Interstellar Travel

Outpost buildings perform many functions, but the primary ones harvest resources like Water or Iron from the planet surface, and create complex resources like Fuel and Stasis.

This scenario has some buildings constructed already, in future you must construct all the buildings you need.

Constructing Buildings

Travel to a planet and construct a water harvester building on the planet's surface.

> The Map Of Worlds is not the most sacred room on a Vault, but perhaps the most practical. With it we see the universe and all spun matter.
>
> The Book of Starlight, Chapter 28

Step 1 Travel to the Planet: Go to the planet's surface with your Exile, and all your resources. Once there, enter the surface view.

Step 2 Assign Laborer: Take the Exile from the ship and place them in the laborer slot on the location display.

Step 3 Select Building: On the building list, select the water harvester entry to start placing it on the grid.

Step 4 Choose Location: Harvester buildings require placement on the grid that covers a resource node. Place the water harvester on the surface grid spot that contains the Water resource.

Step 5 Construct Building: On the build display, select the Construct button. This uses the Iron in the Location Storage to construct the building.

Step 6 Restore Actions: End the turn to restore the Exile's actions.

Continue to Operating Buildings

Operating Buildings

Use the water harvester to gather Water, and the other existing buildings to create Stasis and Fuel.

Step 1 Harvest Water: Select the water harvester to open its display. Select the Operate button to produce Water. Each building operation requires an action spent by the Exile in the laborer slot.

Step 2 Produce Stasis: Select the Stasis Producer figurine to open it. Note that creating Stasis needs Water, Titanium, and CO2. Now that you've harvested Water, all those resources are present at this location.

Operate the Stasis producer like you did the water harvester, and it uses the resources present to create Stasis. Operate it again to create a second unit of Stasis, enough for one Exile to hibernate.

Step 3 Produce Fuel: Operate the fuel producer to create fuel for your return journey. Harvest more Water as necessary, and end the turn to restore the Exile's actions.

Step 4 Return to the Vault: Once you create enough fuel, return to the Vault with the Stasis you created. Transfer it to the Vault Reserves.

Step 5 Begin hibernation.

End Scenario.

Extraction is a vital process, if regrettable. The pious submit willingly, but others resist.

The Ritual of Interstellar Travel

This concludes the introductory scenarios. The next solar system is the first true system of your journey. The Game Concepts section contains a step by step guideline to complete it, but the fundamentals of maneuvering ships and constructing buildings remains the same.

Game Concepts

This section of the manual describes how each individual component of the game functions.

These two pages give a broad set of guidelines to completing a solar system, and completing a full journey of The Banished Vault.

Guide to Escaping a Solar System

After the introductory scenarios, solar systems are randomly generated. The first solar system is designed to introduce you to the game as a whole, without more advanced concepts introduced later.

Your primary goal in each system is to escape before the Gloom arrives, and create enough Stasis to put all your Exiles into hibernation. Turns and Stasis will always be shown to you at the top of the game screen. If you make a mistake, restart the solar system using the button in the top left of your screen.

Step 1 To create Stasis, you need Water, CO2, and Titanium. Look for planets and moons with these symbols to harvest those resources.

Also take note of locations with Iron, to harvest for more building construction.

Step 2 Plan maneuvers to the locations with the resources you need. Remember to bring fuel for the return trip, or for a smaller ship to bring resources to another location.

Step 3 Load the items you need to construct buildings from the Vault onto ships. Constructing a   Stasis Producer requires Alloy, Iron, and Titanium.

> Use Quick Swap to quickly transfer items.

Most harvester buildings are constructed with Iron. Producers and other buildings require a combination of resources. Use the Reference section to determine your resource needs.

Step 4 Add Exiles to your ships. The more Exiles you have in one location, the more actions you can accomplish there per turn.

Step 5 Maneuver your ships to their destinations.

Step 6 Once your ships arrive, begin constructing buildings.

> To better plan your outposts, place multiple buildings before constructing them. Once constructed, buildings cannot be removed.

Step 7 Harvest resources and create Stasis. You need 2 Stasis for each Exile. All resources must be at the same location as a stasis producer to create the Stasis. This may involve shipping resources from multiple outposts to a central outpost.

Step 8 Harvest and create spare resources for the next solar system. Iron and Fuel are crucial, while Water and Titanium are useful.

Step 9 Return to the Vault with your Exiles and resources. Items stored on ships are taken to the next solar system after hibernation.

How to Complete Your Journey

To complete a journey of the game, you must complete four entries in the Chronicle of the Auriga Vault. Inscribing an entry into the Chronicle requires visiting a Hallowed planet and constructing a Scriptorium there. Each Hallowed planet allows only one Scriptorium. Once the Scriptorium is constructed, the entry is written.

Hallowed planets bear this symbol:

Some solar systems do not have Hallowed planets.

After completing a journey, the game unlocks journey configurations for modifying the starting conditions of future journeys.

Tips, Tricks & Efficiencies

There are a few subtleties in The Banished Vault that might not be immediately apparent, and so are collected here to aid more advanced or efficient play.

> *Engines are made functional by Fuel, bodies kept alive by Stasis, and faith upheld by Elixir.*
>
> *The Book of Starlight, Chapter I*

◆ Your journey can hinge on the spare resources you bring to the next solar system. Iron and Fuel are crucial, Water and Titanium are important, and any spare Alloy saves time and travel.

◆ Ships have a different Mass, which affects how efficiently engines generate Energy. Thrust is always the engine's Thrust value modified by the ship's Thrust value.

◆ Planets closer to the sun have a higher Action Restore value, allowing for Exiles to have more actions per turn there.

◆ Use Quick Swap to quickly move an Exile or item from a ship's display to the Vault or location, and vice versa.

◆ Buildings cannot be moved or destroyed once constructed. Place all of the buildings you need before constructing them to ensure your outpost layout is planned carefully.

◆ To plan multiple maneuvers, it can be helpful to plan in reverse. Allocate fuel and resources for the final step of your maneuver, and then the penultimate, and so on. This ensures you have enough resources to achieve every maneuver in a sequence.

◆ The more fuel spent on a single maneuver, the less efficient each individual unit of fuel is. To maximize your efficiency, plan multiple smaller maneuvers, if your Exiles have enough actions to do so.

◆ Exiles with a higher faith better overcome hazards.

◆ The Reference section outlines all building costs and uses.

Auriga Vault

The Auriga Vault is the home of your Exiles and the method of transport between solar systems. It is always located at the furthest location from the sun, and cannot be destroyed by the Gloom.

The machinery of the Vault is vast and ever-changing. It would take many lifetimes to see its extents, and it could not store a catalog of its mysteries.

I see spires that did not exist years ago, and find new passages to old chambers. My memory leads me astray.

Extract 30, dated MMCCX.13599

Chronicle

The Chronicle is a log written by your Exiles over the course of your journey. Once a Chronicle is written, your journey can end. See How to Complete Your Journey.

The chapel of the Chronicle remains inaccessible, suspended above the cathedral of Auriga. We have adapted our methods.

Extract 67, dated MMCCX.64888

Auriga Vault Interface

Select the figurine of the Auriga Vault to open its interface. Here is where you recover the faith of your Exiles, store items to take to the next solar system, fabricate new ships and engines, and begin the hibernation process.

The Vault Reserves stores items and resources for transport between solar systems.

The Crew tab holds your Exiles and Stasis for hibernation.

The Chapel tab is where you place Exiles to recover their faith by consuming Elixir. See Faith for more details.

The Shipyard tab is where you construct new ships and engines. The resources for construction must be located in the Vault Reserves at the bottom of the display. Constructing a ship or engine requires assigning an Exile to the engineer slot, and costs one action.

Additional ships and engines are unlocked by spending Knowledge during hibernation.

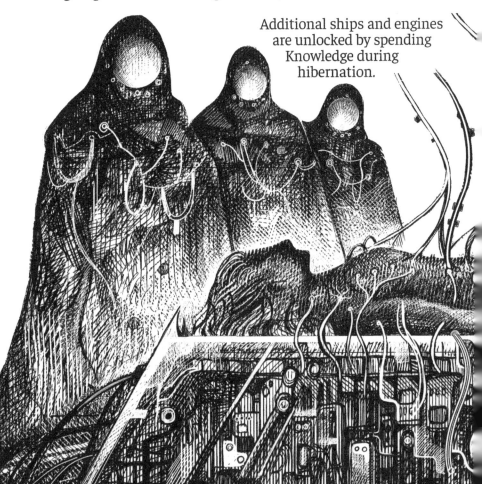

Hibernation

Once you are ready to leave a solar system, begin the hibernation process from the Crew tab of the Auriga Vault display.

Once you enter hibernation, all ships, Exiles, buildings, and items that are not in the Vault or at the Vault's location are lost forever. Items inside ships at the Vault's location are taken to the next solar system.

Each Exile requires 2 Stasis to hibernate until the next solar system. If you do not have enough Stasis, you must choose which of your Exiles to keep alive. Each Exile's faith goes down by one when hibernating.

On the hibernation screen, first choose which Exiles to administer Stasis. Then, you may spend Knowledge on purchasing abilities for your Exiles, or new buildings, ships or engines. Each Exile can only have one ability, but it can be replaced.

Exiles

Exiles are the survivors of the Gloom, and the characters under your control in the game. Once an Exile dies, they are gone forever. If you are reduced to only one Exile, your journey ends.

Exiles are displayed in various locations throughout the game, called slots. Each slot is named, and most allow that Exile to perform actions. Select an Exile or use Quick Swap to move them between slots.

The display shows the Exile's portrait, their faith, and the number of actions remaining this turn.

At the bottom of the main game display is a list of all your Exiles. Selecting them navigates the game to the Exile.

The true population of a Vault is continually recorded, but the records themselves are hidden. Once, such a record was found, but the process of decoding it was not completed for decades.

The Fourteenth Manuscript of Balthe

Items

Items are the various things you will gather, create, and transport in the game. Item slots hold multiple items of the same type. Slots have a limit for how many items they fit.

Select a slot to pick up all items in that slot, or use Cancel to pick up one item from the slot. Use Quick Swap to send a stack of items from the ship display to the location or Vault displays. Some slots only allow a specific type of item, such as engines for a ship or Stasis on the Vault.

The display shows the item's image, the amount of items in the stack, and an indicator of how full the stack is, represented as the white outline around the amount value.

Item stacks are destroyed by picking them up and selecting the Destroy Item button that appears at the top of the screen.

Faith

Faith is an important aspect for each Exile. It is the way Exiles overcome hazards in the solar system, and if an Exile's faith reaches 0, they cannot do any actions.

The Exile's faith is displayed next to this symbol:

Faith dictates how many dice are rolled when you resolve a hazard. The more dice rolled, the higher chance the hazard is resolved successfully.

Elixir is a most wondrous substance. Extract of sunlight itself.

The Book of Starlight, Chapter 2

Over time, an Exile's faith diminishes. When they enter hibernation, each Exile's faith goes down by one. They can also lose faith as an outcome of hazards.

The faith of an Exile is restored in the chapel at the Auriga Vault. Place the Exile in the chapel slot, and a number of Elixir equal to the Exile's current faith plus one.

Ex. If an Exile has 3 faith, it costs 4 Elixir to raise the Exile's faith to 4.

Once the Exile and Elixir are placed, the Exile gains faith at the start of the next turn. An Exile's faith cannot be higher than 6.

Turns

The Gloom pursues you constantly, so your time in a solar system is limited. This time is measured in turns and displayed at the top of the screen. During a turn is when you use Exiles to perform actions.

On a new turn, an Exile in the chapel location on the Vault gains one faith at the start of the turn, if there is enough Elixir in the chapel.

When you end the turn, any ships on turn stops continue their maneuver. All Exiles' actions are set to maximum dictated by the location.

Once the remaining turns reaches zero, the Gloom begins destroying the solar system. Each turn after zero, the planet or region closest to the sun is destroyed, including any buildings, resources, ships, and Exiles.

Actions

Each Exile has an individual amount of actions to spend each turn. Actions are displayed next to this symbol:

Actions are spent on:

Starting Maneuvers
Constructing Buildings
Operating Buildings
Searching for Artifacts
Building Ships
Building Engines

It is impossible to know how long Exile's spend in a solar system, as time is measured from the current star and no longer from the central coordinator orbiting the galaxy.

The Eighth Manuscript of Balthe

Exiles only regain actions at the start of a turn. The number gained is based on their location at the start of a new turn. Exiles at the Vault gain 3 actions, and on ships in space they gain 1.

If an Exile is on a surface or orbit location, they gain actions equal to the region's Action Restore value. Generally, the regions closer to the sun have a higher Action Restore value.

If an Exile has 0 faith, they cannot do any actions. See the Faith section for more.

Solar System Map

The map of the solar system is organized in a tree structure of all planets and major regions of the system, with the Auriga Vault always at the outermost point of the solar system.

There are many locations on the map, which represent stable orbits or points of rest for ships. While stopped at locations you can move Exiles around on a ship, change engines, or transfer items and Exiles between ships.

Surface locations are marked with the square symbol and orbit locations with the round symbol. Some types of planets like gas giants do not have surface locations.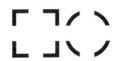

Other locations inside a region are marked with a small cross. Ships can stop at these locations and rendezvous with other ships. Locations on the root path of the solar system are marked with a small diamond. Ships cannot stop at these locations.

Each region has an action restore value, the amount of actions Exiles gain at the start of a new turn, shown next to the action symbol. Near the orbit location, the atmosphere resource of the region is displayed, if any. Near the surface location, the resources available at the surface location are displayed.

Hazards at locations can be displayed in two ways. If a location is unexplored, an open triangle symbol is displayed to indicate uncertainty of the hazard's status. Once a location is revealed, either the open symbol disappears if the location has no hazard, or the full symbol is displayed if it does.

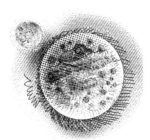

Locations are separated on the map by paths. Paths represent the distance between locations, and can have one or multiple costs to traverse them:

- Energy: All paths have an Energy cost, although it can sometimes be zero. Energy is created by spending fuel with an engine. The Energy cost is the value next to the E symbol on the path.

$$E\ 9$$

- Thrust: Most paths that go from the surface of a body to orbit have a Thrust requirement. Engines produce Thrust, and ships modify the Thrust. The total Thrust must be equal or greater to the path, but it is only a requirement and not spent like Fuel. The Thrust requirement is the value next to the T symbol on the path.

$$T\ 1$$

- Turns: Some paths in between regions of the solar system force ships to stop one or multiple turns. This represents a vast distance of travel time.

- Hazards: Some paths have hazards that must be resolved before the ship continues its maneuver. Movement hazards are shown with the larger symbol, and the strength of the hazard in the center.

Ships

Ships carry Exiles and items between the Vault and the locations of a solar system. Ships are constructed at the shipyard on the Vault. Different ship types have different configurations of Mass, travelers, cargo, and Thrust modifiers.

The first ships were towers taken from the tallest cathedrals and lifted into the heavens. The first orbits still, a small shrine in the darkness.

The Book of Starlight, Chapter 9

Select the figurine of a ship to open its interface. If a ship is moving, you can view its interface but not make any changes to the Exiles or cargo until it stops moving.

If multiple ships are in a location, all colocated ships are listed next to the display. Select a button in the list to set the display for that ship. Transfer Exiles and items between ships by picking them up and selecting the desired ship's button in the list.

Ships require an Exile in the navigator slot to perform maneuvers. The navigator is also who resolves any hazards the ship encounters.

Other Exiles can be placed in the ship as travelers, located below the navigator. The number of traveler slots varies between ship types, from zero to four.

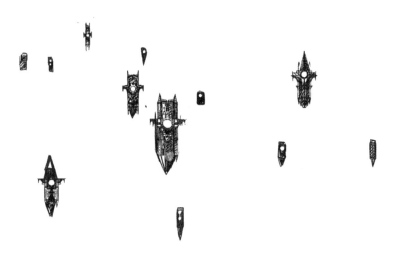

Ships have a condition value, which can be reduced by hazards. The value starts at 5 when a ship is created. If the condition value is reduced to 0, the ship and all its travelers and cargo are lost.

Items in the ship's cargo are in the middle of the display. The number of item slots varies between ship types. Items and Exiles have no bearing on the Mass of a ship when calculating the Energy of a maneuver.

Below the cargo are the main components and information for performing maneuvers with the ship. The engine slot is where you assign the engine for the ship to use in a maneuver. Once the engine is set, the total Thrust value of the ship is computed.

Fuel sets the amount of fuel for the maneuver. You cannot set more fuel than exists in the cargo of the ship. Below the fuel amount is the current conversion ratio. This value will show you how much Energy will be added to the maneuver for the next unit of fuel spent.

Once the fuel and engine are set, the Energy range is computed. The amount of Energy generated per unit of Fuel decreases as more Fuel is assigned to a maneuver. All of the fuel assigned is consumed for the maneuver, even if the ship has more than necessary.

Engine Efficiency and Ship Mass are the values that compute the total Energy for a maneuver, along with fuel. See the Energy Calculator for more. Engine Thrust and Ship Thrust are added to produce the final Thrust value.

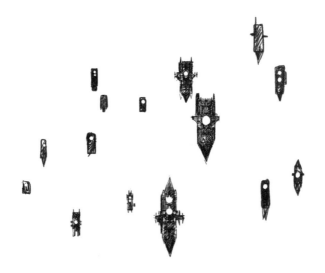

Maneuvers

Maneuvers are how you move ships to different locations in the solar system.

To start a maneuver, first select a ship, then hover over a destination location on the map. The total cost of Energy and turns are displayed over the destination. Select the destination to confirm the maneuver's path.

A maneuver cannot be started if the ship does not have enough Energy or Thrust capability, displayed at the bottom of the ship's display. If any portion of the maneuver cannot be completed, the relevant value of the path on the map appears with a red highlight.

Adjust the amount of fuel spent to produce as much Energy as you need. The amount of Energy a unit of fuel creates decreases as more fuel is spent on the maneuver. An engine with a higher efficiency or a ship with lower Mass improves the fuel to Energy conversion.

The engine's Thrust is added to the ship's Thrust to create the total Thrust. The total Thrust must equal or exceed all Thrust requirement values in the maneuver.

Once the values for the maneuver are correctly set, select Start Maneuver to launch the ship. Once a maneuver is started, it cannot be changed or stopped.

If a ship enters a turn stop marker during the maneuver, it stops at that point until the next turn. If a ship enters a movement hazard, it stops until the hazard is resolved.

The motion of a vessel through the lesser heavens is unusual. The ships are bound to an ocean with strong currents, but the ships can drift on a wave and visit any island in an archipelago. We navigate those currents which run deepest.

The Fourth Manuscript of Balthe

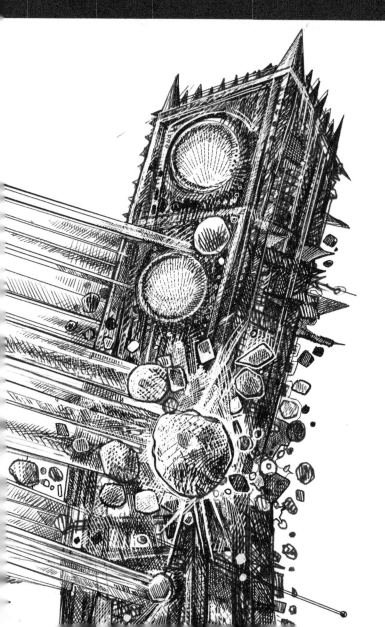

Hazards

Hazards represent dangers to your Exiles in the solar system. Hazards are resolved by a single Exile and their faith. Each hazard has a difficulty, ranging from 2 (easiest) to 6 (hardest).

> *The heavens are cruel, a clockwork mechanism of indifference. Each sunrise is beautiful and horrifying.*
>
> The Book of Starlight, Chapter I

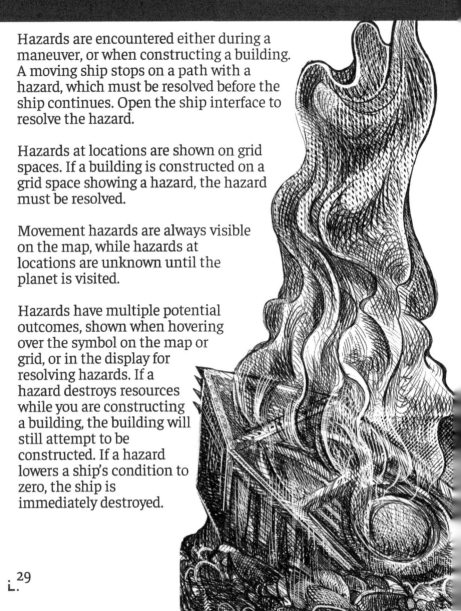

Hazards are encountered either during a maneuver, or when constructing a building. A moving ship stops on a path with a hazard, which must be resolved before the ship continues. Open the ship interface to resolve the hazard.

Hazards at locations are shown on grid spaces. If a building is constructed on a grid space showing a hazard, the hazard must be resolved.

Movement hazards are always visible on the map, while hazards at locations are unknown until the planet is visited.

Hazards have multiple potential outcomes, shown when hovering over the symbol on the map or grid, or in the display for resolving hazards. If a hazard destroys resources while you are constructing a building, the building will still attempt to be constructed. If a hazard lowers a ship's condition to zero, the ship is immediately destroyed.

Resolving Hazards

When you resolve a hazard, the hazard display appears in the center of the screen, showing the hazard values and dice rolling display.

When resolving a hazard, a number of dice equal to the Exile's faith are rolled. The goal is for any of the dice rolled to have a value equal or higher to the strength of the hazard.

Ex. The Exile's faith is 3, and the hazard's strength is 5. Three dice are rolled, and the values are 2 3 6. The Exile overcomes the hazard.

Once you are ready, select Roll Dice to resolve the hazard. Once the dice stop rolling, the hazard's outcome is presented to you.

This table describes the percentage of a successful outcome, given the number of dice rolled against a target hazard difficulty.

Hazard Difficulty	Dice Rolled / Faith					
	1	2	3	4	5	6
2	83%	97%	99%	99%	99%	99%
3	66%	87%	96%	98%	99%	99%
4	50%	75%	87%	93%	96%	99%
5	33%	55%	70%	80%	86%	96%
6	16%	30%	42%	51%	59%	76%

Location Interface

Once a ship visits an orbit or surface location, select the figurine on the map to open the location display. Here you construct and operate buildings, and gather artifacts.

To return to the map view, select the Return To Map button at the top of the display at the right.

At the top of the display the atmosphere of this location is shown, if it has one. The action restore value is how many actions an Exile regains at the start of the turn. The Ships button opens the display for any ships at this location.

At the bottom of the display is the location cache, which stores items at that location. Items used for construction and operation of buildings must be stored here.

Each planet starts with some resources in its cache, depending on the number of resource nodes the location has. These resources are freely accessible.

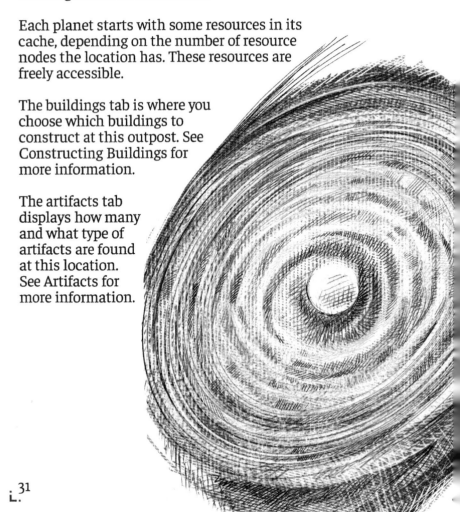

The buildings tab is where you choose which buildings to construct at this outpost. See Constructing Buildings for more information.

The artifacts tab displays how many and what type of artifacts are found at this location. See Artifacts for more information.

Location Grid

In center of the location screen is the grid where buildings are constructed.

A planet's surface is a treacherous and hostile creature, granted a willpower by gravity and solar radiation. Our outposts are like a leaf on a raging river, soon pulled under and dashed against a distant shore.

The Ritual of Interstellar Travel

Not every space allows a building to be placed on it. When placing a building, the game interface will alert you to how many spaces are invalid for placing the building. Buildings cannot be placed on grid spaces that other buildings occupy.

Grid spaces can hold resources, which are spaces harvesters of that resource type must be built on. Some spaces have a hazard symbol and the strength of that hazard. If a building is placed over a hazard space, it must be resolved before the building is constructed.

Some resources on the grid have a depth rating, from 1 to 3. Before harvesters can be built on these spaces to gather resources, the resource must be revealed first. This requires the construction of a Resource Scanner matching the depth of the resource.

Ex. Resource Scanner 2 reveals depth 2 resources.

Resource Scanner buildings can be constructed anywhere on the grid.

Constructing Buildings

Buildings are constructed on Orbit or Surface locations. Each building has a footprint in grid spaces, and some have a resource requirement. An Exile is required in the laborer slot of the location display to construct a building.

The method of establishing an outpost is highly advanced. The primary intent is the establishing of a mission, and later a colony. The secular purpose of colonies varies greatly but the seed always begins the same. Vaults began as replicators for these seeds, with additional purposes added as the centuries passed. In the current era, ships are furnished with the ability to seed outposts, and the process has become commonplace.

The Fourth Manuscript of Balthe

To construct a building, select its button in the building list, then select a location on the grid to place the building. You may rotate the building before placing it.

The building is placed, but not constructed yet. You can still remove unbuilt buildings by selecting the Cancel Construction button. You can also continue to place buildings before constructing any, to better plan your outpost.

To construct a building, the required resources must be present in the Location Cache. If there is a hazard, it must be resolved before construction. This costs one action for the Exile in the laborer slot.

Once a building is constructed, it cannot be moved or deleted.

Harvester buildings require the relevant resource for construction. Most resources are present on specific grid spaces on the grid, and the building must occupy that space. If the resource is present in the atmosphere, the building can be constructed anywhere.

Converter buildings take resources as inputs and produce other resources. Additional buildings provide unique effects.

Orbit buildings have special restrictions. An Orbit Structure building can be constructed anywhere, but all other orbit buildings must be built adjacent to an orbit structure.

Operating Buildings

Most buildings can be operated, those which harvest resources or convert resources from one type to another. An Exile is required in the laborer slot of the location display to operate buildings. Select the building's figurine to open it in the location display.

If a building is a harvester, it requires no inputs. Otherwise, the input resources must be present in the Location Cache to operate the building. Select the operate button to harvest resources, or convert the input resources to the output resources. This costs one action for the Exile in the laborer slot.

Outpost structures are both densely organized and distant from one another. Time is spent traveling between structures and reconfiguring them for unseen complications.

Arrival and departure rites should be meticulously followed, even when traveling alone or with mechanical aid.

The Ritual of Interstellar Travel

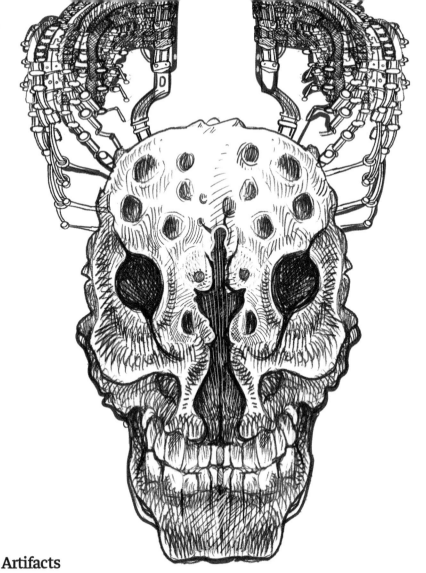

Artifacts

While your Exiles are hibernating in between solar systems, you may spend Knowledge to unlock new buildings, engines, ships, and abilities for your Exiles. To unlock these items, you need to gather artifacts from locations in the solar system, and return them to the Vault. The artifacts are then converted into Knowledge.

To find artifacts, you must have an Exile in the laborer slot on the location display. Select the artifact tab and select Search for Artifact.

Most locations have artifacts available to gather. Artifacts vary in the amount of Knowledge the Vault rewards.

Energy Calculator

The Energy Calculator is a tool used to calculate the Energy range of
a ship, without using the ship display or needing the resources.
Access the calculator from the button at the top of the screen.

The calculator has three adjustable sliders, for Engine Efficiency,
Ship Mass, and Fuel. The Engine Efficiency and Ship Mass values are
found on the ship display, or in the tooltips for the items. The fuel
slider is how much fuel to spend on a maneuver.

To use the calculator, set the engine efficiency slider to the engine's
value, and likewise the Ship Mass slider to the ship's Mass value.
Then adjust the fuel slider, and observe the resulting Energy value
displayed on the last row.

The value indicated by the red line in the Energy slider is the
resulting Energy produced.

System Survey

With the construction of stellar surveyor buildings, it is possible to see the resource composition of the next solar system on your journey. Each stellar surveyor reveals the status of three resources in the next system.

This status is seen in the Survey display, accessible from the button at the top of the screen. A resource status, from highest to lowest, can be Generous, Sufficient, Sparse, or None.

Restarting Solar Systems

You can restart solar systems using the button at the top of the screen. Depending on the configuration of your journey you may restart any number of times, once per system, or not at all. Restarting has no other effect on the game.

Exile Abilities

During hibernation you may spend Knowledge to purchase abilities for your Exiles. These give positive effects and bonuses for the duration of your journey while that Exile is alive. Each Exile can only have one ability, but that ability can be replaced.

Journey Configuration

After completing a journey, configurations are unlocked to adjust the starting conditions of future journeys. These can increase or decrease the difficulty of a journey. Those configurations are:

Solar System Restarts
Solar System Difficulty
Resources on Vault
Fuel on Vault
Number of Starting Ships
Number of Starting Exiles

Advanced Maneuvers

Frequently in the game, a complex movement of multiple steps must be calculated before starting the first maneuver.

The most efficient method of moving through space is to only use heavier engines when necessary, such as landing on planets. Any engine can move a ship through space, even if the resulting Thrust is 0, so the most efficient engine available is the best.

A potentially useful method to construct a multi-step maneuver of space travel is to consider each segment in reverse order. Each step in this context is a single maneuver, generally paired with changing an engine.

Ex. Leaving a planet and going to its nearby moon: this is a multi-step maneuver with 3 steps: planet liftoff, transit to moon, moon landing.

To calculate how much fuel you need for all three maneuvers, start with the last one, landing on the moon. Inputting the values into the Energy Calculator you can determine the fuel needed for the moon landing step.

Repeat the calculations for each step, noting how much fuel is needed in total. Once all the steps are calculated, the total amount of fuel needed for the sequence of maneuvers is determined.

Navigating ships is a highly complex procedure, with no shortage of deaths associated with it. After too many priests died in the first ships, adjustments were made in the composition of travelers.

The Book of Starlight, Chapter 19

The primary tradeoff of ship maneuvers is fuel efficiency to Exile action efficiency. As more fuel is spent in a single maneuver, the less Energy is generated per unit of fuel. This makes it less efficient to move a great distance in one single maneuver, and more efficient to use multiple maneuvers.

However, each maneuver requires the Exile in the navigator slot to spend an action. In this situation, fewer maneuvers are ideal for conserving actions.

Reference

Resources

Elemental resources in the first column below are harvested from planets. Complex resources are created using buildings at an outpost. All resources can be put in a stack of up to 9 like items.

CO2
Used for Stasis and some buildings.

Alloy
For advanced construction.

Iron
Used to construct many buildings and to create Alloy.

Elixir
For rejuvenating the faith of your Exiles.

Titanium
Used to construct many buildings, and for Stasis and Alloy.

Fuel
For powering the movement of your ships.

Silica
Used for Alloy, Elixir and buildings.

Stasis
For keeping your Exiles alive during hibernation.

Methane
Used for Elixir and engines.

Water
Used for Fuel, Stasis, and ships.

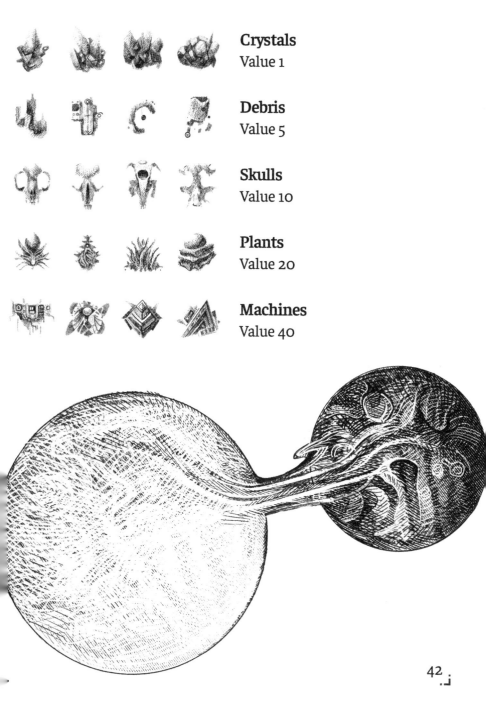

Artifacts

Artifacts are gathered from planets and other locations which provide Knowledge when returned to the Vault. Each location has one kind of artifact to be found. Artifacts cannot be stacked.

Crystals
Value 1

Debris
Value 5

Skulls
Value 10

Plants
Value 20

Machines
Value 40

Buildings

Buildings are constructed at locations. Harvesters gather resources from the location. Converters create new resources from inputs. Other buildings provide various effects.

A * on a building's name means it must be unlocked during hibernation.

Resource Key

C - Carbon Dioxide
E - Elixir
F - Fuel
I - Iron
M - Methane
S - Silica
T - Titanium
W - Water

Surface Harvesters

	Cost	Outputs
CO2	2 I	1 CO2
Iron	3 I	1 Iron
Methane	1 I	1 Methane
Silica	3 I	1 Silica
Titanium	1 I	1 Titanium
Water	2 I	2 Water

Orbit Harvesters

	Cost	Outputs
CO2	1 T	2 CO2
Methane	1 T	2 Methane

Surface Converters

	Cost	Inputs	Outputs
Alloy Producer	2 I, 2 T	1 I, 1 T, 1 S	1 Alloy
Elixir Producer	2 I, 1 T	1 S, 1 M	1 Elixir
Fuel Producer	1 I, 1 T	1 W	3 Fuel
Reverse Sabatier*	1 I, 1 T	2 W, 1 M	3 CO2
Sabatier*	1 I, 1 T	3 C	1 Water, 1 Methane
Stasis Producer	1 I, 2 T, 1 A	1 W, 1 T, 1 C	1 Stasis

Orbit Converters

	Cost	Inputs	Outputs
Alloy Producer*	3 T	1 I, 1 T, 1 S	2 Alloy
Elixir Producer*	2 T	1 S, 1 M	2 Elixir
Fuel Producer*	2 T	1 W	4 Fuel

Other Surface Buildings

Other Surface Buildings	Cost	Description
Artifact Surveyor*	1 A, 3 S	Adds five more artifacts for gathering at this location.
Power Generator*	3 A, 2 C	Increases the action restore value of this region by 1.
Resource Excavator 1	1 I	Reveals all resources at depth 1.
Resource Excavator 2*	3 I	Reveals all resources at depth 2.
Resource Excavator 3*	5 I	Reveals all resources at depth 3.
Scriptorium	2 A, 2 E	On a Hallowed planet, used to write an entry for the Auriga Chronicle.

Other Orbit Buildings

Other Orbit Buildings	Cost	Description
Stellar Surveyor*	1 T, 1 C, 1 F	Reveals the status of three resources in the next system.
Surface Observatory*	1 T, 1 F	Reveals the terrain and hazards on the surface of this planet.
Large Orbit Structure*	2 I	Allows building orbital buildings in adjacent grid squares.
Orbit Structure	1 I	Allows building orbital buildings in adjacent grid squares.

Ships	Cost	Travelers	Mass	Cargo	Thrust
Sparrow	1 Alloy	0	1	1	1
Swift	1 Alloy, 2 Water	1	1	1	1
Nightjar	1 Alloy, 4 Water	2	1	1	0
Crake	2 Alloy, 1 Titanium, 2 Water	1	2	2	0
Shrike	2 Alloy, 1 Titanium, 6 Water	3	2	2	-1
Francolin	2 Alloy, 2 Titanium, 2 Water	1	2	4	-1
Rail	3 Alloy, 2 Titanium, 4 Water	2	3	4	-1
Petrel	3 Alloy, 2 Titanium, 6 Water	3	3	4	-2
Merganser	3 Alloy, 2 Titanium, 8 Water	4	3	4	-2
Eider	4 Alloy, 4 Titanium, 2 Water	1	4	8	-2
Avocet	4 Alloy, 4 Titanium, 4 Water	2	4	8	-2
Stork	4 Alloy, 4 Titanium, 6 Water	3	4	8	-3
Serpentarius	5 Alloy, 4 Titanium, 8 Water	4	5	8	-4
Heron	5 Alloy, 6 Titanium, 6 Water	3	5	12	-4
Ibis	5 Alloy, 6 Titanium, 8 Water	4	5	12	-5

Engines	Cost	Efficiency	Thrust
Margay	1 Alloy, 1 Methane	220	1
Planiceps	2 Alloy, 1 Methane	205	1
Chaus	1 Alloy, 2 Methane	190	2
Oncilla	2 Alloy, 2 Methane	175	2
Caracal	1 Alloy, 3 Methane	160	3
Lynx	2 Alloy, 3 Methane	145	3
Diardi	1 Alloy, 4 Methane	130	4
Serval	2 Alloy, 4 Methane	115	4
Pardus	2 Alloy, 5 Methane	100	5
Panthera	2 Alloy, 6 Methane	85	6

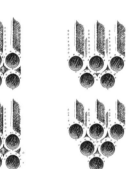

Notes

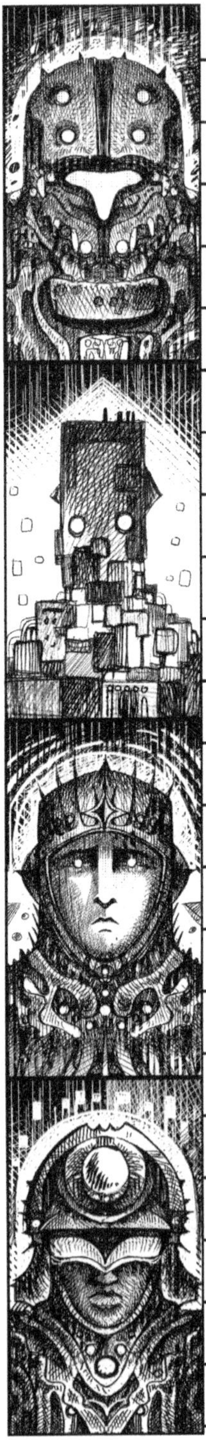

Notes

Notes

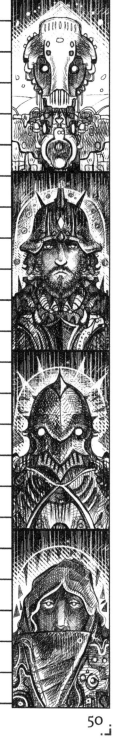

Notes

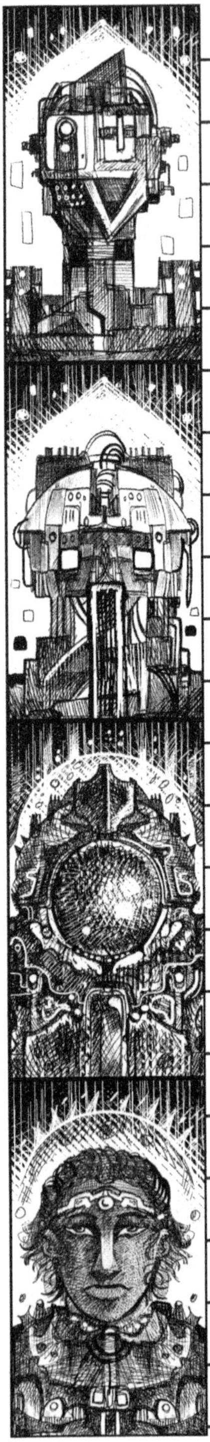

Notes

Notes

Notes

Notes

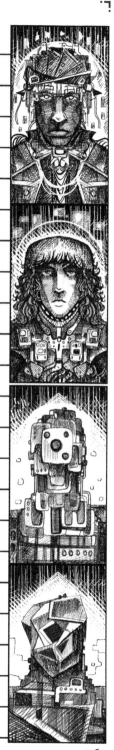

Notes

Printed in Great Britain
by Amazon